David Pelletier

The Graphic Alphabet

Orchard/New York

A SCHOOL BOOK CLUB SPECIAL EDITION

ISBN 0-590-12199-5

12 11 10 9 8 7 6 5 4 3 2 1   7 8 9/9 0 1 2/0

Printed in the U.S.A.   37
First Scholastic printing, September 1997

The text of this book is set in 24 point New Caledonia.
The illustrations are computer-generated images reproduced in full color.
Book design by David Pelletier.

For Hsien-Yin Chou, Luci Hitchcock, and
Zbyszek Kaluzka ~ who got me through it.   Thanks.

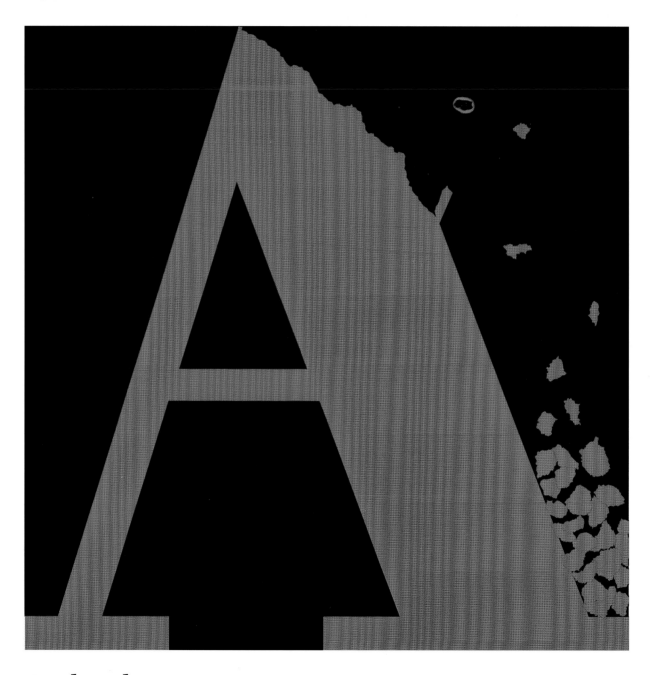

Avalanche

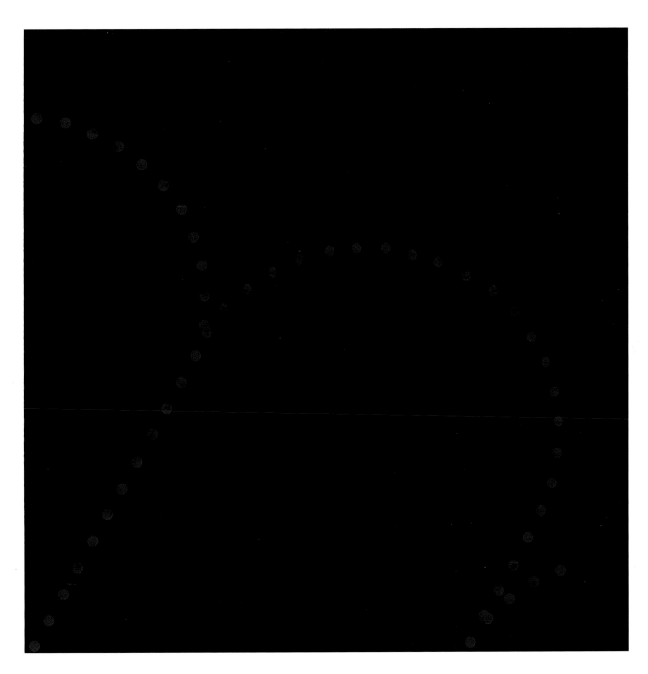

Bounce

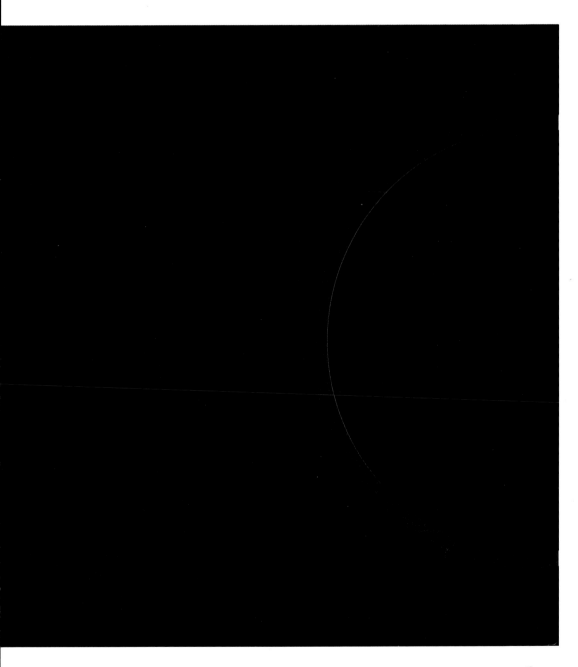

Circles

Devil

Edge

Fire

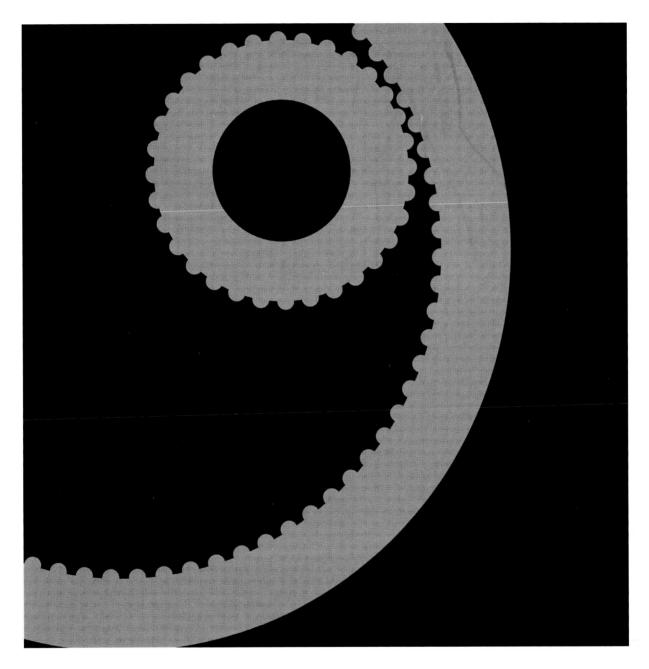

Gear

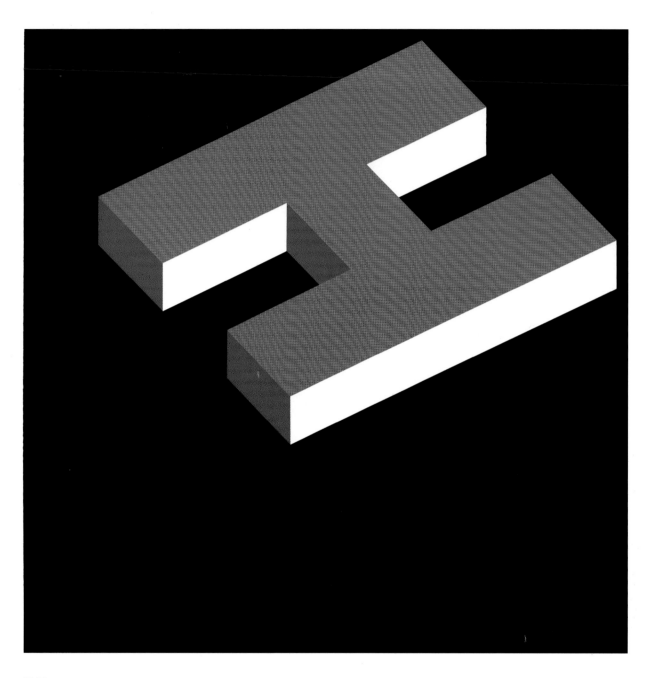

Hover

Iceberg

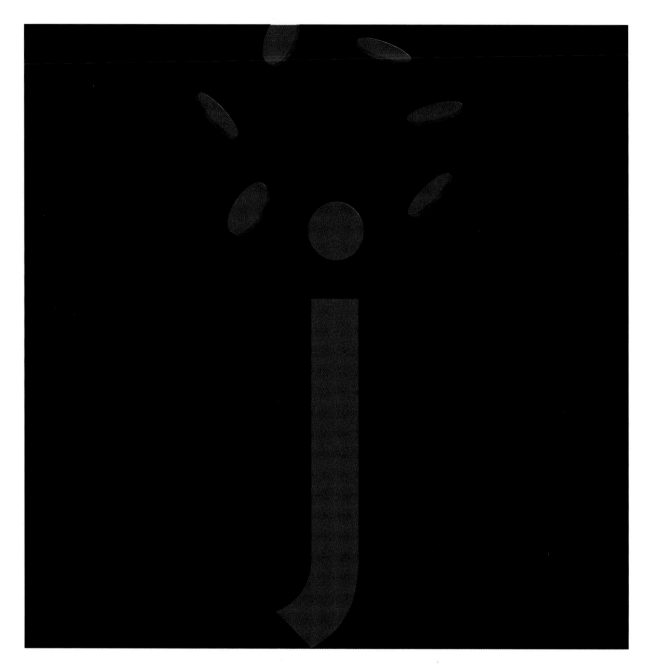

Juggle

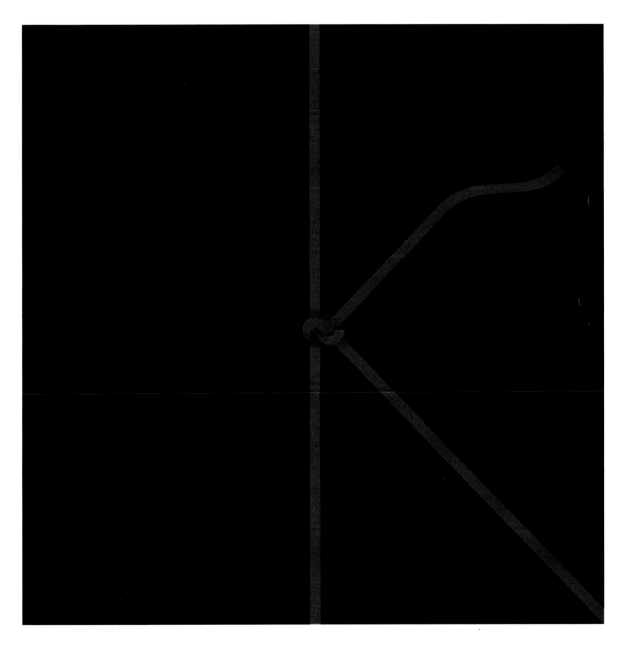

Knot

Lines

Mountains

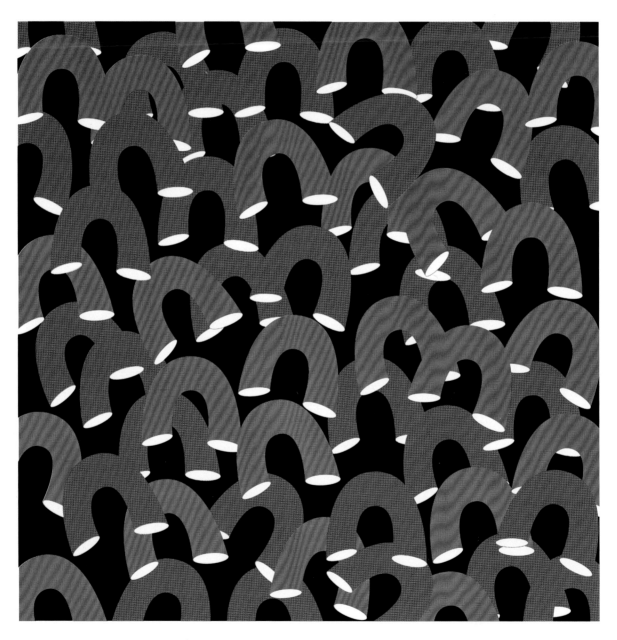

Noodles

Ornaments

Pipe

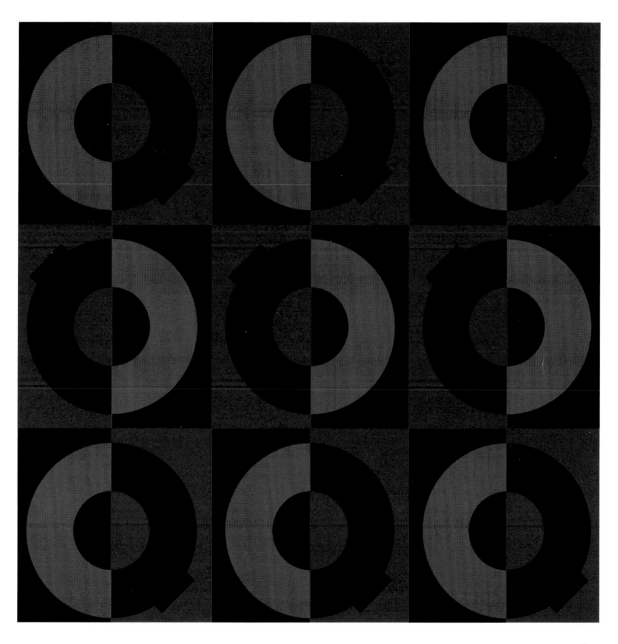

Quilt

Rip

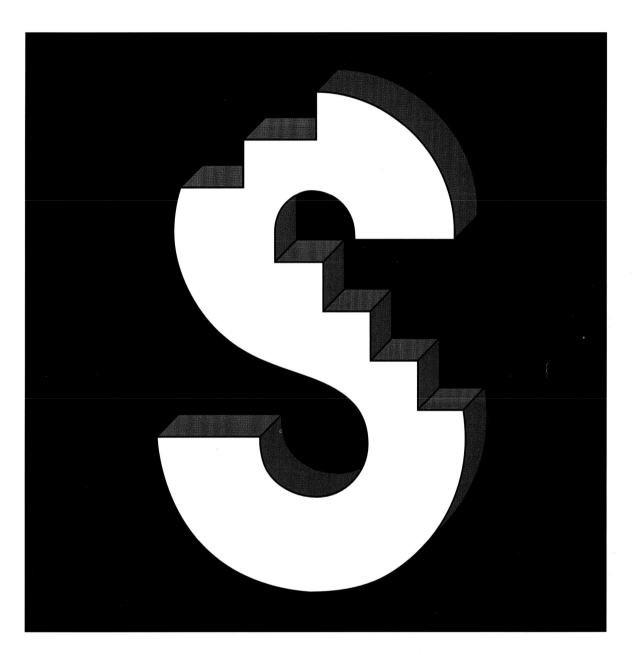

Steps

Trip

Universe

Vampire

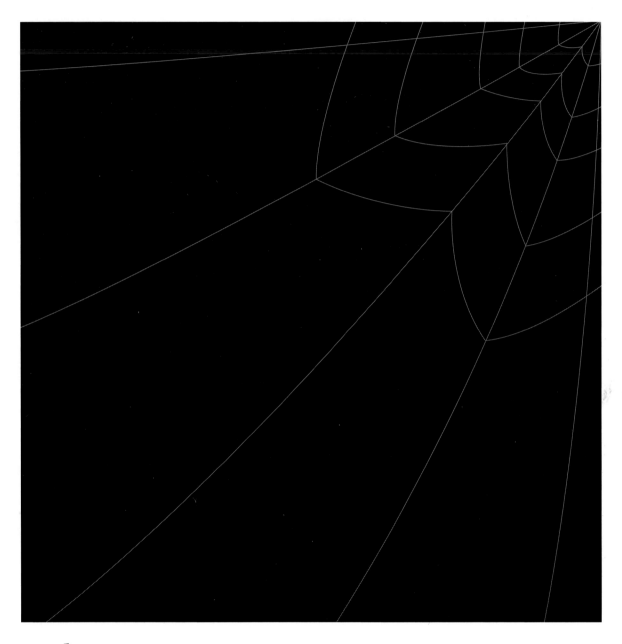

Web

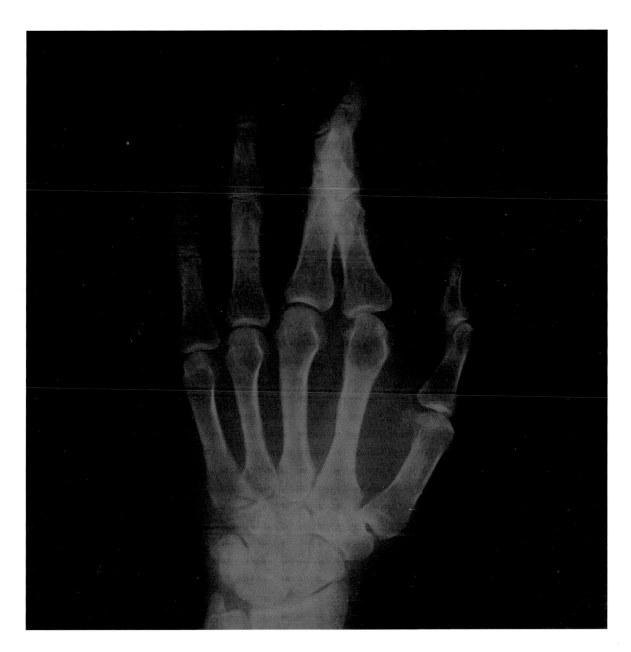

X ray

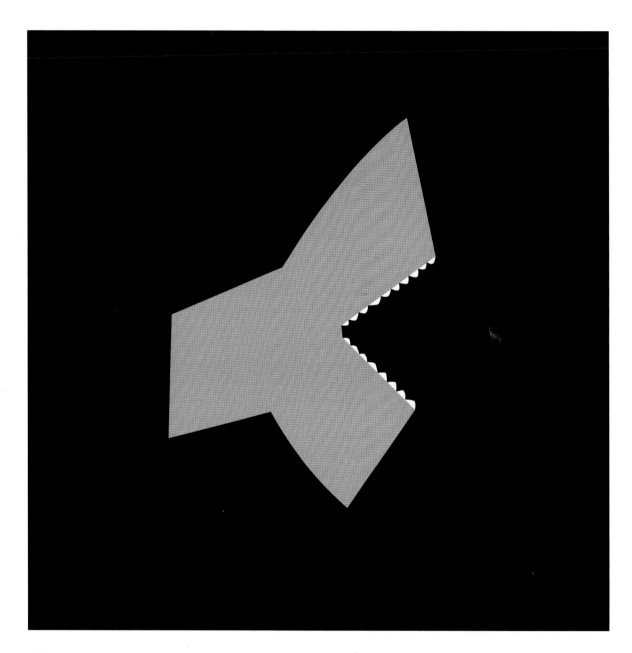

Yawn

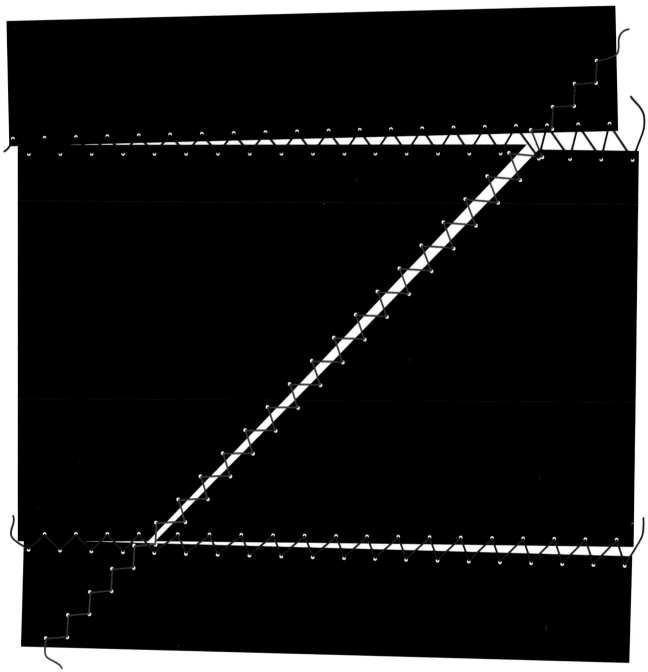

Zigzag

David Pelletier is a graphic designer living and working in New York City. This, his first book, grew out of a long-standing interest in letterforms and in the relationship between image and meaning. Expanding on a traditional form for children, the alphabet book, he decided that "the illustration of the letterform had to retain the natural shape of the letter as well as represent the meaning of the word."

The Graphic Alphabet is the result.

Thank you to Neal Porter for his tenacity, and to Jeremy Sherber for his assistance in the production of this book.